Dedication ~ Thank You, God

For amazing grandchildren ~ Christa, Cora, Thane, Lance, Keely and Jadon
For 7 year old Tyler Langley who loved his family and God's Amazing World
For the privilege of teaching God's beautiful children in New Mexico, Oregon, Colorado,
and Hawaii, as well as in Zimbabwe & Togo

God's Amazing World introduces preschoolers to the ecology of a variety of the world's geographical regions. Kids will enjoy the amazing multi-sensory world of rhythmic verses and quilted illustrations. The landscapes and animals were created completely of fabric by Judy and her daughter-in-law, Kimberly.

A special thanks to Audrey Burchyett, Judy's world traveling friend, who added the detailed stitchery including the eyes of the animals and the faces of the children.

Thanks also to Sandy Wray, a Colorado friend, who photographed the illustrations for *God's Amazing World* as well as for, *Celebrating the Seasons with Granddad/Cozy Days with Grandmother.*

For arranging the song, *God's Amazing World*, I am grateful to my Montana brother-in-law, Mark Langley.

To order additional copies of this book, contact:
Xlibris
844-714-8691
www.Xlibris.com
Orders@Xlibris.com

ISBN: 978-1-4257-6345-9 (sc)

Print information available on the last page

Rev. date: 10/25/2023

GOD'S AMAZING WORLD

Written by Judy Langley

Illustrated by Kimberly Langley and Judy Langley

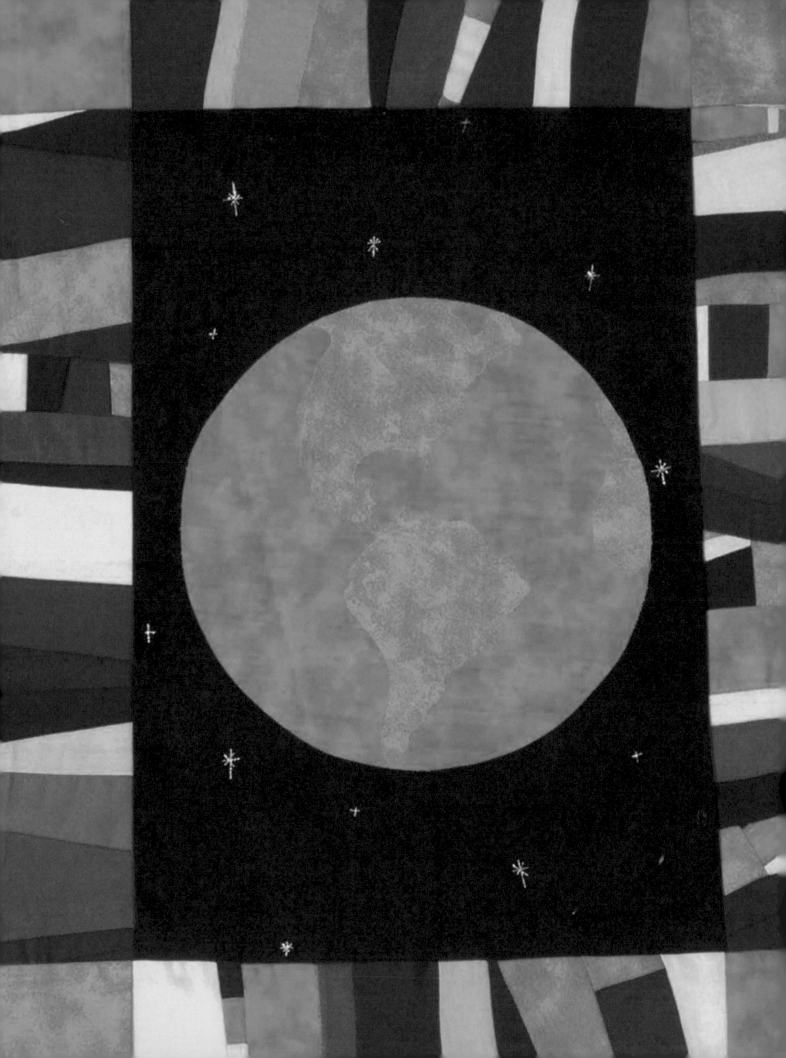

God made
the world
with
loving care...

Raccoon
Woodpecker
Forest
Bear.

Starfish
Pelican
Ocean
Whale...

Ostrich
Elephant
Grassland
Quail.

Cactus
Rattlesnake
Desert
Fox...

Penguin
Polar Bear
Arctic
Ox.

Beaver
Chickadee
Mountain
Pine...

Monkey
Crocodile
Jungle
Vine.

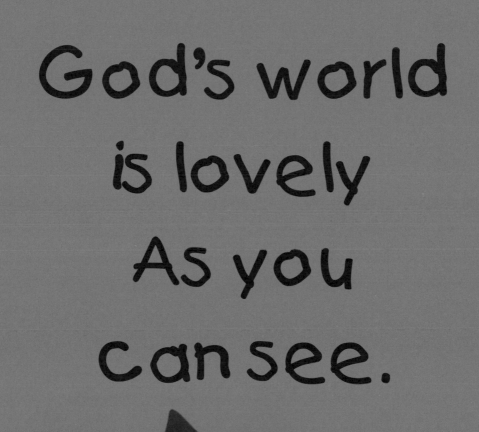

God's world
is lovely
As you
can see.

God loves
His world.
He loves
you and me!

God's Amazing World

Arranged by Mark Langley

Music and Lyrics by Judy Langley

Fun Activities

1. Sing *God's Amazing World:* As you sing, act out each animal with actions and hand motions. Discuss how amazing God made the world, including us! Talk about what we can do to take care of our world. (Start at home, in your backyard, in your neighborhood, in your city, etc.)

2. Design a Mobile: Cut out a large rectangle from poster board. Write one region of the world on the card and decorate with pictures of the vegetation and scenery of that region. Draw and cut out animals from the region. Punch 3 holes on the card and 1 in each animal. Hang animals from string or yarn. (See example below.)

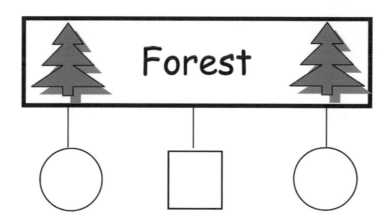

3. Make a Scrapbook: Find pictures of animals in wild life magazines, in coloring books, and on the internet. Add a heading for each region and glue pictures of animals from the different regions.

4. Play Games: Call out the name of an animal and have children guess the region. Call out a region and have children list the animals.

5. Collect Art Books that Show How to Draw Animals: Practice drawing them. Hang your art work on a bulletin board or on the fridge.

Author/Illustrator Judy Langley

Author Judy Langley, a Texan by birth, graduated from Wayland Baptist University and married her high school sweetheart, Phil Langley. Judy taught school in New Mexico, Oregon, Hawaii, and Colorado. They served in Zimbabwe and Togo in international missions and in church planting in Colorado, New Mexico, Hawaii and California.

Judy published 6 mission adventure books for preschoolers and children with New Hope Publishers— the 5 book Land Far Away Mission Series and *God's World and Me from A to Z*. She also published, *Celebrating the Seasons with Grand-dad/Cozy Days with Grandmother* with Xlibris. Judy enjoys writing, singing, playing the piano, riding 4-wheelers in the mountains of Colorado and traveling with her husband. Judy's 6 grandchildren continually inspire her to write.

Quilter/Illustrator Kimberly Langley

Quilter/illustrator, Kimberly Langley, was born in Duncan, Oklahoma. She attended Oklahoma Baptist University where she met and married Anthony Langley. Most of their children were born in Western Europe: Christa and Cora in England, and Thane Edward in Germany. Lance Anthony was born in Colorado Springs. Kim has worked at various jobs during their travels, including after school care at a private school in Germany. Kim enjoys traveling, interior decorating, cooking, singing, crafting, collecting antiques, gardening, and training her 3 dogs: a Labrador, a Weimaraner, and a Malamute. Kim and Judy designed and created the quilted illustrations for *God's Amazing World* from fabric!

Printed in the United States
by Baker & Taylor Publisher Services